Unbound

Alyssa Langworthy

BookLeaf
Publishing

India | USA | UK

Made with ❤ on the BookLeaf Publishing Platform

www.bookleafpub.in

www.bookleafpub.com

Dedication

to myself, at every stage of this journey, in every universe, in all forms.

Preface

This collection includes poems written throughout many phases of my life. Writing has gotten me through every up and down, every love I've learned and lost. My pen has been there in the trenches of the deepest depressions and the highs of light resurfacing to life. Welcome to the ride. I leave these musings here, not necessarily feeling unraveled, but *unbound.*

Acknowledgements

to everyone who's been on this journey with me: named and unnamed, appreciated and unappreciated, turmoil and treasured

Special thanks to Tama "Mama T" Brisbane for seeing me at fourteen years old, and truly seeing *me* in all of that raw, untapped potential.

1. 27 Club

A polaroid portrait eclipses into existence
A blacked out blur of birthday cake candle smoke and
haze set the scene
Cheers-ing myself with shots of Jameson
Chasing my liquor
with with handfuls of happy pills
that never seemed to ever make me happy.
Ironic, don't you think?

A pretty princess sitting alone in the VIP
at a birthday party for one,
doing baselines off the dancefloor,
trying to find God at the bottom of the bottle.
You'd think I'd have gotten the message
the first time.
Fade to black

I woke up in the twilight hours my first day of 26 by
miracle
with no memory of finding my way home,
laying face down on my bedroom floor,
empty bottles like confetti on the hardwood.

I don't know how I've gotten so lucky with so many

chances at this life.
A fact I have to keep reminding myself
when I feel empty
and abandoned,
like a laundry list of RSVPs and well wishes
without a single familiar face to walk through the door.

Childish for me to be this big age
throwing a tantrum with big girl money and
big girl party favors.

I spent most of 26
battling between trying to remember and wanting to
forget.
Watched as my entire support system unraveled itself
like gift wrap before my eyes,
beating myself up for fighting so hard for people who
never really showed up for me in the first place,
let alone at a
fucking birthday party.

By the time 27 showed its face,
I had left LA in a cloud of dust,
the world shut down around me.

I told myself the world had to stop
for me to finally learn how to sit in my own fucking

stillness,
soaking in my Saturn return
in solitude.

I've learned the hard way
how heavy an instant can feel --
the magnitude a single snapshot of life can carry.
I don't know how I've gotten so lucky with so many
chances at this life.
But, I am thankful to get the chance to try and learn
the why

2. Paloma

We sit in the backyard of an airbnb
The summer incense of Coppertone and bud burning
between your fingertips
The warm Palm Desert night
blowing on our necks like a favorite lover
The sky a deep shade of purple as the earth swallows the
sun

You pour me a paloma
More tequila than grapefruit
More tajin than salt

Illuminated in the spark of your bic lighter
A flight of doves soar around your bicep
The same tattoo you share with your sisters, in memory
of your late father
You took me to visit his grave on the drive out of orange
county

I didn't know this roadtrip was the beginning of our end
Wouldn't see the road signs until months after i missed
your exit
Our friendship built on the intimacy of shared secrets
Finding solace in the fact we both knew Don Julio better

than we knew our fathers
You, the forever boy with the sunset skin and golden
hour smile
Protected by the charm you wore like rosary beads
The brightest star in any galaxy
But
even mosquitos will lure themselves
into the light of a death trap

I tend to forget that light can be blinding
That darkness can hide underneath it
Looming like dimples framing a picture perfect smile
Using pretty words to tell you how to hate yourself

sometimes we can't recognize abuse until
We are already halfway dead
Not knowing our limits until we are pushed past them
One morning i woke up realizing i was
Paper-craning myself into smaller versions of someone i
didn't know
Found myself asking you to stop being the helping hands
Folding me in on myself
I was so tired of being gaslit i set myself on fire to prove
a point
Burning bridges because i could no longer participate
in paying my own death toll

I think about that night
In the air bnb in palm springs
Like a polaroid that keeps developing
Your name still burns in the back of my throat like
patron without the lemon
I think of us playing bartender and the tattoo on your
shoulder
And i wonder if you even realize
Paloma means dove

I don't know if I can offer you olive branches
But i know that my heart is finally healing
Filling the cracks from our fracture with gratitude
Appreciating the years of our friendship
For what they were
Forgiving you for projecting your own inner demons
Onto my insecurities
Letting go of the pain i've been holding onto
Releasing, like doves at a wake

3. Tearstained Glass Closet

When the sun shone,
kaleidoscope rainbows
shattered and refracted the glittering future
you've convinced yourself that you can't have.

You live your life within your
tear-stained-glass-closet,
hugging yourself straight-jacket tight.
The ultimate Houdini,
the bait-and-switch,
the subtle subtext in screaming bold
begging to be seen – seemingly too afraid to actually do
it.

Virginia Woolf in sheep's clothing.
Too afraid of your own reflection to
learn the shape of confidence without restriction.
Too consumed with the circus charade
and staged stand-ins.
A lover's lie like venom in your kiss.
Sinning in secret,
finding the truth serum on her lips.

You're all hail mary's and soliloquies these days.

A lot of hollow words
for the girl with the golden voice,
for the muse plated in fool's gold.
For the Gatsby of it all,
but nothing Fitz.

Nothing seems what it is.
Nothing feels as good as these what-ifs –
the fantasies behind a smoke screen of fallacies.
The Man behind the curtain is always a girl
who can't say what she wants.
Can't make her love life a spectator's sport.
Can't play the game,
but is somehow still hunted.
Haunted by drunk texts and half-slurred speeches,
half-truths and limo tire screeches.
Hollowed out in Hollywood;
strung out on starlight.

Protecting yourself with the shell of a human you sell to
the cameras.
Shell casings glitter on the hardwood floor.
So tired of being shot at, you started calling the shots –
even at the expense of the girl you could be.

The life you could have,
if you accepted the daylight and basked in the glory,
lifted yourself out of this predisposed casket,
stopped taking the prescribed silence,
because the salve isn't soothing anymore.
Can't heal the harm when you're allergic to the remedy.
Can't keep ignoring the wound
pretending the gaping hole in your chest
isn't the elephant in the room.

You don't owe us anything
But, we see you.

4. Coda

Da capo al coda: (in music),
to go back to the beginning
tracing each delicate step
until reaching the designated finale,
where the melody gracefully bows out
with its final, enchanting refrain.

There are songs I can't hear
without feeling the ghost of your hand in mine.
There are lyrics I can't sing along
without feeling your heartbeat in the basslines.

When I told you
you made beautiful music out of me,
I thought we were a song with no end.

Saw us a never ending playlist,
always finding the right song to send.

Your soul hovered in harmony with mine,
humming hymns in perfect pitch.
Learning the religion in your hips with each switch.
Your lips like fingertips against the steel strings

of my neck.

But now,
I'm just a hollow body left in a hollow bed.
An extended play cut short,
left for dead in a deafening silence.

No horns and brass to play our funeral march.
No beat left in this flatline.
Haunted by radio stations
and grocery store mixtapes.
There hasn't been easy listening in years,
lost in the swell of the sound waves
that remind me of you.

Only finding comfort in the tracks of my own tears.
Trying to forget that the record's scratched
or warped;
I can't remember which.

There are songs I can't hear
without feeling the ghost of your hand in mine.
There are lyrics I can't sing along
without feeling your heartbeat in the basslines.

But, I cannot continue
to let my voice piano into a whisper.

I refuse to let the dissonance of the distance
you put between us sour the songs
I've loved so deeply.

I cannot stay stuck on repeat forever:
trapped behind these bars,
locked in this loop.
Don't you remember
when you used to call me
songbird?

You, my love,
can keep
the space you asked for.
You can keep the memories
as they fade out into the ether.
I'll even let you keep the score.
But, you do not get to keep
my melody.

5. [Redacted]

I dressed up as Buffy the Vampire Slayer
for "celebrity crush day"
at the high school I work at
Leopard print dress
Leather jacket
And kick ass boots

I took a look
Stood back from my floor length mirror
And said
Holy shit Batman
I look like [redacted]

[redacted] was my college ex girlfriend
Who (it had not donned on me before getting dressed
this morning)
was obsessed with Buffy Summers
Even wrote her honors thesis about
vampirism as a metaphor for chronic illness

[redacted] was every white nerdy incel boy's idea of a
Mary Sue
The blue print of your boyfriend's version of a manic
pixie dream girl

Pastel pink bleach fried bob and Jeffrey Campbell boots
Crushed velvet mini skirt that rose up when she bent
over

[redacted] was the first girl I ever had the confidence to
kiss in public sober
She only drank Pabst Blue tall boys and craft brewed
ciders and sours
I was used to frat parties and arms full of tally marks
counting down countless cheap ass vodka shots
I was used to the glitter and debauchery depicted in
Ke$ha music videos
I was intimidated by how fucking cool she felt
A stark contrast to the imposter syndrome and teenage
dirtbag energy I embodied

I started watching Buffy because she told me how much
she loved the show
Told me how influential the character was on her
growing up
And I wanted to get to know the foundation of her more
intimately
So I watched
Saw Sarah Michelle Gellar kick vampire ass
Envied her 1997 time capsule closet
Identified with Willow
Witnessed the first major lesbian love arc play out on

television
I have to be honest the special effects do not hold up
But it was the first time I ever fell in love with someone
by proxy
To love something so fiercely simply because the person
you love
Loved it first

[Redacted] was the first time a connection
felt so automatic
I didn't know love could be so simple
But leave it to me to over complicate things

I find myself this morning, nearly a decade later
Standing in front of my full length mirror
In what I can only call [Redacted] cosplay at this point
And
I look so fucking hot

I'm so happy to be in a place
Where I can allow myself to think about
How happy we were
When we were
And not allow myself to spiral
Because [redacted] wasn't my first
hand in heart break
But the knife of her cut the deepest

Today I can look at myself
dressed like Buffy the Vampire Slayer
See the ghost of you in my reflection
Say out loud to myself
"Holy Shit Batman I look like fucking [Redacted]
And I can shrug
And move the fuck on with my day

6. Subtly Sapphic Sad Chicks

I thought Taylor Swift was gay before it was "cool"
You hated that I speculated about her sexuality.

But, you also liked to make truly haunted works of art out of the
Decapitated baby doll skulls you unearthed from their thrift shop graves
So...you can get your kicks
and I'll get mine

We had an on-and-off again
Will they, won't they
Schoolgirl situationship that
Rivaled teenage dramas of the early 2000's on the WB
Not the CW, the WB

Subtly sapphic sad chicks
Putting the alt in alternative lifestyle
You told me you'd never date a man again
Told me you couldn't stomach the thought
Told me how badly you wanted to kiss me
At the Hillcrest bus stop at sunset after I got my nose pierced

On Friday the Thirteenth

I was putty in your hands
Like thrown clay at the wheel
Letting you mold me at the whim and mercy
of your fingertips

The first girl who ever gave me those bluegreen bedroom
eyes
Whose laugh felt like daybreak
Like warmth returning to blue lips

When we eventually fell out of orbit
I phoned home like ET
Missing the gravitational pull of our chaos

You said you'd met someone
And that he was the real deal
Told me he treats you nicer than any man before
That he's such a good guy
I don't know who you were trying to convince more

I say I'm happy for you. I say I miss you
You ask if we can still be friends
And I lie, reply yes
You know my affliction for self-harming behaviors

We stop texting
I unfollow your account
You still view my stories.

7. Puppet Love

When I heard your new man proposed to you
At the Jim Henson Studios on La Brea
A part of me wanted to fight
Not only does that MAN
Have my ex girlfriend
He has the AUDACITY
to taint HOLY GROUND
I swear to fucking god I'm over you
But it's the salt in the wound I can't rub in like salve

If Janice and Miss Piggy were queer
That was us
You and your hippie dippie vegan bullshit
And me fat and as fucking fabulous as ever
High femme fatale suns
With floppy felt puppet dad joke moons
The Lion and The Bull
Two forces of nature
With silly goose vibes
But vibes are never enough
To build an everlasting love

I can still feel the electricity
From the first time you held my hand in the park

The mayhem you commenced the first time you told me
you "loved my goofy ass"
The two of us playing and making out to the
music of our adolescence
Lighting the wick of "us" with your Bic lighter
Meeting you *felt*
Like meeting my dream girl
Your instagram handle was
@ manic-pixie-dream-ghoul
My beloved monster,
I don't really know which one of us
Was the monster at the end of this book

And I've turned the page
I swear to god i've turned the page
I've navigated to the end of the labyrinth
That was losing you
The world fell down around me
No pitch of helping hands offering me direction
All to come to realize
"You have no power over me"

the best gift you have ever given me was letting me go
What your absence lacked in gentleness
Wisdom came in bounds

I really hope you are gushing over your betrothal

The way I used to gush over you
I pray you never experience his betrayal
The same way I pray I never allow myself to accept
crumbs and potential
as monuments of desire
again.

I may not be a man
I may not even be a muppet
But I am (for maybe the first time ever)
Myself – in all of my flawed monstrous gloriosity

8. Missing You

I'm standing in the back of a bar
one hundred
and ninety-six thousand miles
from home
missing a girl who isn't mine to miss

I mix Jameson and cigarettes with regrets
pink twinkle lights reflect off the cheekbones
of new friends with pretty faces
whose kisses are not quite as kind as yours

Another *Groundhog's Day* night
reliving these nightly reruns on bar stools
downing doubles and chasing with my attempts to find
myself in strangers
when I'd rather make myself at home in your cupid's
bow

I remember our first date
we turned two hours into eternity
with you time tends to stop
remember we shopped at your favorite thrift stores?
talked about all the shitty punk bands we both loved
long before we knew each other

You: short skirt, cotton candy colored hair
Me: in *awe* and ripped jeans
jittering with nerves and butterfly belly

We are both too preoccupied with life for full-time
commitments
chasing our dreams in opposite directions
two planets orbiting around each other
never quite finding the right timing
the universe pulling us together
and then reminding us of our magnetism
repelling like kitchen magnets in the hands of
should-have-been lovers

I'm standing in the back of a bar
one hundred
and ninety-six thousand miles
and an entire ocean from you
finding comfort in rose-colored shot glasses
taking shots to the head instead of the heart
alcohol might not be an anesthetic, but damn can it
numb
keeps the wounds clean and my vision blurred
I see the resemblance of your face in hers

There's an Elliot Smith song plucking away in the
background

the same song i sang you for Valentines Day last year
I keep finding pieces of you
scattered across cities in foreign countries
like some sick scavenger hunt
where ex never *really* marks the spot, does it?
I keep stumbling out of bars getting caught up in this
entanglement
and i'm tired of being a puppet begging you to pull on
my heartstrings

There is a beautiful girl
here
in this bar
one hundred
and ninety-six thousand miles
and an entire ocean from home
asking me to make out with her under the starless sky in
the streetlamp light
the moon reflecting off the river Liffey

And maybe she isn't you
but she's reminding me
that you are not mine to miss

9. breaklights

Los Angeles never felt like home,
but you loved the way she held my foot to the gas
never seeing the redflags in the brakelights.
both of us too fucked up to smell flesh against asphalt
knowing there are no happy accidents.

We were toxic and intoxicating.
a whirlwind romance
blown over by the time the jacarandas were bare,
the purple blooms like ashes
in our aftermath.

We were doomed from our first date.
you took me to Hollywood Forever.
we walked among the mausoleums.
you said there was something so poetic
about seeing stars in the ground
instead of the floodlit heavens.

It never rains in Southern California,
but you showed me it sure does snow.
taught me how to drink away this love drought,
bumping bass lines off of dance floors
both of us praying for The Big One,

playing in the fault lines of our old wounds
finding our friction tectonic
trying to *make* love in the City of Angels and still
coming up synthetic;
no wonder leaving felt like dragging my own corpse up
Sunset.

We were an imperfect storm:
comfortable in the chaos
thinking the eye of the hurricane was the safest place to
find respite
trying to drown out the sirens
knowing the tsunami would wash us away with the
turning tide
tired of waking up to a cold front and a cold shoulder

We were promised sunshine and palm breezes.
I didn't know about June gloom.
I didn't know about the purple blooms laying themselves
to rest
marking the graves of every street corner I kissed you
on.
I didn't know to look for the redflags in the brakelights.
I didn't know to brace for impact.

10. Violets

I

I've tried to find myself in the breeze
a fluff of dandelion seed sent wayward to the sea
searching for a safer place to nestle into soil
a sapling with no intention to simmer in summer heat
a precious peach not built for a blistering son

I always knew there was no way to root under these
conditions
the probability for my ability to propagate has always
felt scarce
the family tree I branch from is rotted to the heart
tended to by the grimmest of reapers
this cycle of slash and burn is a scorch beyond endurance
this acidic soil has singed my skin
seared from the heat of a thousand sins

I search for an eden of alkaline vines and fig trees
foraging for forests full of foliage and fruits like mine
I long for beds of honey sweet earth where my roots will
take
I envision meadows glistening in the morning's dew
pastures of perennials on rolling hills

babbling brooks with banks of baby's breath
and violets as far as the eye can see

II

violets have been tucked inside the pockets of lovers like
mine for centuries
pressed between pages of the sapphic storybooks
history has always wanted to tear the pages from
our love stories banned and burned at the stake
I wonder what color the flames were?

My love has no right budding from this family tree
where we shed layers of bark like shrouded secrets
pick at the open wounds we can't seem to heal
I have always been made to feel like the weight of
deadwood
teetering in the balance, waiting for the impending doom
of lightning's crack
knowing that the axe comes at the first sign of what they
see as disease
how was this ever meant to feel like home?

I stand alone
rooted in my own convictions

gardens growing at my feet
the genesis of my own eden of freedom
where we will carry pockets full of purple posies
celebrating the deaths of cycles and abuse
we are the children who've been divorcing our parents
for eons
apples falling farther from the limbs that never
embraced us in the first place

I am choosing to take the crown from this tree
strip it of all the lies hidden in the leaves
weaving garlands of wildflowers in the glow of golden
hour
knowing that royalty will always shine in the shade
of violet

11. Phase

Life keeps teaching me the same lessons over and over
again
I guess that means I haven't been doing much learning
I keep repeating these same patterns, returning to cycles
I keep thinking I've broken
I keep writing the same poem, reciting into an
echochamber
never taking the hints I keep leaving myself in idiom
taking turn of phrase at face value
never really examining how close it hits to home

I never really feel myself until I am loved by another
either friend or lover I tend to get lost
phasing into you and never truly into myself
completely codependent under the guise of fierce
independence
morphing
contorting my body into boxes I knew I could check for
other people
making the same dumbass decisions, just with a new
haircut
called it reinventing myself
called it adapting
gave it a positive spin

never realizing it trauma response
constantly on the run from who I am
who I've been
trying to be someone else you could love
laying myself by the wayside
and painting your hands in red

before I can forgive the hands that've harmed me
I have to first learn how to forgive myself
for falling into the same traps set specifically for me
falling with a heavy heart and thick skull
squeezing every rock trying to find a diamond
never not once putting the same pressure on my own
neck
too afraid to look harder in the mirror
frightened of finding infinity
calling everyone else out their name
before learning the weight of my own
hatting its bitter taste on my tongue
choking on this reflection, this shadow
realizing the truth is really fuckin hard to swallow

I am exhausted
tired of having the same lesson stuck on repeat,
but never being able to make it stick
constantly pulling the swords from my back
never taking the time to lick the wounds clean

having the audacity to be surprised when they sting
letting myself bleed out in the name of pride
waving my ego instead of a white flag

This body does not know surrender
only the dogma of fight or flight
waxing and waning between relationships
forgetting even the moon is still whole even when she
sees herself a sliver

12. and sometimes the air colors itself around you

and sometimes the air colors itself around you
the fuschia and tangerine of sunset
draw the warmth from your throat
you try to catch your breath
feeling the ballast of a moment pass beneath you
the weight of the earth below your feet
you've never quite noticed its gravitational pull

never quite felt a part of this place
never quite felt your humanity
seemed too heavy
too burden
your helixes feel like helium
always trying to pull you towards the sun

your feet like cinderblocks
heavy and cemented in their stubborn
too comfortable in the shadow
high off the scent of fresh asphalt
dragging your heels down every path
paved with you in mind
you've always been the devil on your own shoulder

your best critic and your worst friend
a toxicity for the ages

aren't you tired of being the first hand to harm this
body?
knowing too well how bloody the cangage can be
forgetting a simple slight of tongue can be corrosive
seemingly hellbent on your own destruction
but for what?
why?
you know the joy of having a belly full of fireflies
why keep them tight inside a mason jar of limit

the all too familiar feeling
of water filling your lungs
the weight of your own self loathing
sitting on your chest
drowning in the ocean you've cried yourself
scrambling towards the surface
seeing the light break through the crest of waves
getting caught in the undertow
tumbling through days into weeks into months
battling your every instinct to fight back
learning that sometimes you just have to unclench your
jaw
relax your fists
let yourself feel your bones smack against rockbottom

sit in the surf trying your best not to wallow in it

you wash up onto shore
the second week in October
the crisp Astoria autumn blowing against the damp of
your cheek
the fuschia and tangerine of sunset
draw the warmth from your throat
you try to catch your breath
feeling the ballast of this moment pass beneath you
the weight of the earth below your feet
for the first time you notice its gravitational pull

and you understand that a dark day can come as easy as
high tide
but looking out into the kaleidoscope of dusk
you remember that your light can bend without breaking
and your misty eyes can make magic refractions
and sometimes the air colors itself around you

13. Salt

It is said that salt water is the cure for everything
tears, sweat , the sea
I believe, wholeheartedly, that this is fact
I have felt it, tasted it, known it
I have seen its medicinal virtues, tested and true
My grandmother must be in on it too
the way she over salts the water before she breaks in the
pasta
lets it bubble and boil
sticks her face over steam
as if the saliferous vapors will toil away her troubles
as if they can evaporate into the fog clinging to her
thick-rimmed glasses
I think she believes that they can disappear like ghosts
but ghosts seem to stick around longer than expected in
this house
I haven't seen her cry since my grandfather passed
but I know how salty that starch water is even after the
noodles
have let their guard down and gone soft
I wonder if she sees the correlation
sees his reflection in every bubble bursting in the red pot
on the stove
I wonder if her heart still simmers.

She stopped smoking two years ago, a year after his
death
I wonder if she's replaced the tar in her lungs with salt.
She tells my mother she envies my ocean view
apartment
in a city four hundred and ninety-three miles and eight
hours away
She lives in his house
within the walls of a mortuary dedicated to his memory
lined with photographic evidence of his existence
he was an avid photographer
tried to capture every moment, every memory
even when his mind couldn't develop the polaroids as
quick as he longed for
they still hang there, framed in dust
I wonder how much of it is made up of particles of his
skin
I can't imagine how painful of a reminder this home is
She spends her days in her garden just like she has my
entire life
She now tends to the row of rose bushes lining the walk
to the front door
where she spread his ashes
alone, in silence
She's allergic to roses.
I wonder if she's cried
I wonder if she's discovered the saline oceans hiding

behind her eyes
waiting for a crack in her damn to break
but she is too damn strong for all of that sissy crying and
shit
so she sweats over her garden
sweats over the stove
day dreams about ocean breezes and salty sea air
I tell her it tastes just like the pasta water
in the red pot
on the stove
she tells me
I guess salt water is just salt water
and I can't tell if it's just the condensation
but there are streams rolling off the frames of her glasses

14. speed bump

Just because the scars on your wrists have faded doesn't
mean that they were never there.
Just because your bones have healed doesn't mean you
were never broken.
Just because you've dyed your hair and dyed your hair
and then cut it all off anyways,
doesn't mean you aren't who you were before the bleach.

Just because you stain your face with cosmetic warpaint
before you walk out of the house
doesn't make you any less warrior at 4AM behind
keyboard,
all sweatpants and smudged eyeliner
in the periwinkle halo of laptop light.

You are complex
with history carved into your skin
tick marked and organically tattooed
never forget the days when the pain was so real
you had to split open vein and show the world your
crimson

scars heal
memories fade

but never forget the progress you've made
you are five years removed from the day you carved
initials into your bark
Five years from the days you let razor blades kiss and
leave teeth marks in your skin
five years from fifteen and scared shitless

remember that girl
she will always be a part of you
she is a bend in your river
a wind in the road
don't ever call her speed bump
don't forget *her*
she may just show her face in your reflection one day
and you need to know her better
than she will tell you
she knows you

15. Cycles

you find notes of your mother in your voice
you've inherited more than just her temper
be the soft she never felt she could be

you have your father's eyes
always fixed on the heavens
always scanning the skies for some sort of sign
praying over your own exit plan

the thing about genetics is
they are strong even when they shouldn't be
you have to find the beauty in the cycles
or they will swallow you whole

be your mother's mistakes
be your father's favorite drink
wear it well
remind him of the things he used to love before he knew
you

be strong
because cycles have the tendency to become black holes

just remember

the resemblance

is uncanny

16. groomed

I didn't realize I was coming home to a ghost town / I
forgot how haunted these hallways could feel / they say
shame is a silent killer / I've heard silence equals death /
so, what happens when the bodies begin to talk?

I'm tired of being the damning bones buried in the back
of your closet / mourning the life I could have had
without your interference / struggling with the fact that
there were times you painted me golden.

Looking back through this rose-colored looking glass /
truly seeing how distorted those funhouse days were / I
am ashamed / to have been fourteen and manipulated by
a grown man / to have had you open this space that felt
like a home I'd never known / to finally feel safe enough
/ but the reality / the fact / was that
that couldn't have been anything further from the truth.

When you saw my face for the first time in years / no
wonder you looked like you'd seen a ghost / saw me a
phantom / a bad habit you thought you kicked / buried
in a past you dug down deep / prayed to your God to let
you sleep at night / how dare you.

The voices in my head blame me for believing in you /
for trusting you / for being a fucking fool at fourteen / I
should have known better, but how / you know I never
got to be a child / even though I was one.

You always told me how mature I was / how grown I
seemed / how comfortable I made you feel talking about
things grown men shouldn't discuss with children / and
while you may have never made any physical advances
with me, whatever you want to calls this, call it
inappropriate / recalling conversations that make my
skin crawl / you should have called me a cab and a
therapist / instead of spinning me in a web I wanted no
part of.

You made me believe that you would never, ever do
anything / to compromise your family / the job you
loved / and the bonds you were building with your
students.

I wonder what would have been if I had been prettier /
thinner / if I would have fallen at your feet / like other
girls my age / just called it a schoolgirl crush / how close
was I to being prey rather than plaything?

I wonder what your wife said when she found out / I
wonder what you told your daughters / I wonder how

you've told the stories of the girls whose photos you've
hung proudly in the classroom you've kept for fifteen
years / I wonder how it feels / to see your past come
back to haunt you / in real time.

Are they giving you real time? / Are they taking your
license to teach? / Your ability to be around minors? /
Are you now a registered sex offender?

I hope / you feel that knot in your stomach / twist like a
knife in your back / I hope that if you feel like girls
coming forward / with their truths is betrayal / you
remember how you taught us secrets don't make friends.

You taught us to write our truths / to put them on a stage
/ to use our experiences as / fuel for our art.

I don't think you realized how well some of us were
listening.

17. just friends

I hate you for the fact that you led me on
But more so for the fact that you swear you didn't
I hate me for letting you in,
For letting you break down my walls
And letting you reach places I didn't even know myself
I didn't even know myself until I met you
And at the age of fourteen it was easy
To love you
Easy to let you strip layers of my sheltered soul
Like the petals of flowers all those other girls tossed at
your feet
"he loves me, he loves me not"
You never loved me
You were only looking for an easy fuck
Searching for other girls bodies in the eyes of house
party living room floors and empty beer bottles
You found love pressed between bed sheets with
walking-self esteem issues clad in glitter and stilettos
But you'd never touch me
Because I was your best friend
More than just friends, more like your counselor
You'd tell me about your dad
I'd tell you about my mom and how she swore we were
together, but we weren't

You'd dump all your baby mama drama on my shoulders
And we swapped dark secrets like first kisses
Cried on each other's shoulders like second base
This was our intimacy
You use to tell me that I knew you better than anyone
But now it's like I barely know you at all
But I think I know you better than you know yourself
You've found a new love
A walking self-esteem issue clad in glitter and stilettos
The definition of insanity is doing the same thing over
and over again
And expecting a different result
I don't understand why you think this one will be
different
When it's always the same girl just wearing a different
shade of skin
Just a different shade of lipstick sticking to the lips she
sticks other men's dicks in
You've been cheated
And you've been back stabbed
I can feel the scars in your eyes
Like fear
Like hope, praying this one will be different
I watched as you hid tears like truths in the dark corners
of your chest
I watched as you searched
 for other girls bodies in the eyes of house party living

room floors and empty beer bottles
watched you sing whiskey lullabies to their drunken
corpses
watched as your masochistic tendencies turned into a
lifestyle choice
running in on them like she ran out on you
you don't get it
I loved you
And I'm different than all those other girls
I would never hurt you
I would never hurt you like she did
I'd hope you know me better than that
I'm not going to apologize for this
For being open and free
And willing to spill my heart's bucket full of tears for
you
But, when your new girlfriend spills yours
I don't want to have to say I told you so
I just want you to know
I never intended for us to end up like this
Like strangers
I haven't spoken to you in months
And this hurts just a little bit more than heart brake

18. blood

scabbed knees
dried and picked at
open, fresh
coagulate and clot
sprayed and splattered
taste like metal, like iron
irony
flesh fresh to the bone
broken
torn
open wound
pooling
in the stained street
the scent
 never leaves the nose
never leaves the carpet
never leaves the bedsheet
never leaves the frays in the denim
the scabbed knee
the stabbing
the crime scene
the carnal
the rage
the fear

the shame
the bleed
the evidence
the life
the living
the dead
the in-between
the blood pumps until it doesn't
life is beautiful until its not

www.ingramcontent.com/pod-product-compliance
Lightning Source LLC
LaVergne TN
LVHW021249200726
843509LV00012B/1608